Bob Marley
Songs of Freedom

The Bob Marley Foundation would like to thank its
Executive Director, Neville Garrick, for his collaboration with
Hal Leonard Publishing on the production of this songbook.

Special thanks to Rita Marley, Sharon Marley, Cedella Marley,
Ziggy Marley, Stephen Marley, Rohan Marley, Robert Marley,
Karen Marley, Stephanie Marley, Julian Marley, Kymani Marley,
Damian Marley, Makeda Marley, Cedella Booker and
Michael Hylton, Esq. for keeping Bob's music and message alive.

Photographs by:
Adrian Boot (all except pages listed below)
Bob Marlcy Foundation Archives - pages 2, 20, 82, 175
Arthur H. Gorson - page 14
Peter Murphy/Claire Hershman - pages 77, 208
Mike Putland - page 72
Neville Garrick - pages 88, 203

Hal Leonard Publishing Corporation
7777 West Bluemound Road P.O. Box 13819 Milwaukee, WI 53213

INTRODUCTION

I didn't see my father as much as I wanted. He didn't have a normal "nine to five" job where you could look forward to him coming home every day — and then put him through total stress. No, we had to wait months at a time to see both Mummy and Daddy (actually we call Mummy "Maw"— kinda southern, don't you think?). And you can imagine how stressed they would get — remember now, it's eleven of us.

We all know how much a boy needs his father. But what about the daughters? The love you feel for him when he's there is so strong. He's your protector, your shield, your strongman. If a kid messes with you, you call your dad. He came to my school once when I told him a girl was teasing me about him being a rasta. I wouldn't cry in front of her, but I cried to him. I pointed out the girl, and he called her over and told her not to trouble his daughter. She then asked for an autograph and he gave it to her. I asked him "why you do dat? Now she thinks you like her." I wonder if he's still laughing.

The memories of the time a daughter spends with her father are cherished. There is a part of my heart reserved just for those memories. And the times we shared were not only precious, they were essential to me. It has been said that if a father is righteous, he helps to mold a young girl's soul into the spirit of a woman. My father was a righteous man.

The pain I feel now that he's not here with us has made my love for him even stronger. I would do anything to have him back. I'm sure we all would. Just to see him smile, to hear his voice one more time. But my father has left us with a strong legacy. I don't mean just me and my brothers and sisters, but all of us.

In each and every one of us there is a little piece of his love that keeps us singing. Singing these songs of freedom.

Cedella Marley
May, 1992

CONTENTS

AFRICA UNITE

Words and Music by Bob Marley

AFRICA, UNITE,
'CAUSE WE'RE MOVING RIGHT OUT OF BABYLON,
AND WE'RE GOING TO OUR FATHER'S LAND.

HOW GOOD AND HOW PLEASANT IT WOULD BE,
BEFORE GOD AND MAN, YEAH,
TO SEE THE UNIFICATION OF ALL AFRICANS, YEAH.
AS IT'S BEEN SAID ALREADY,
LET IT BE DONE, YEAH.
WE ARE THE CHILDREN OF THE RASTAMAN.
WE ARE THE CHILDREN OF THE HIGHER MAN.

AFRICA, UNITE,
'CAUSE THE CHILDREN WANNA COME HOME,
    YEAH, YEAH, YEAH.
AFRICA, UNITE,
'CAUSE WE'RE MOVING RIGHT OUT OF BABYLON,
AND WE'RE GROOVING TO OUR FATHER'S LAND.

HOW GOOD AND HOW PLEASANT IT WOULD BE,
BEFORE GOD AND MAN,
TO SEE THE UNIFICATION OF ALL RASTAMAN, YEAH.

AS IT'S BEEN SAID ALREADY,
LET IT BE DONE, YEAH.
 I TELL YOU WHO WE ARE UNDER THE SUN.
WE ARE THE CHILDREN OF THE RASTAMAN.
WE ARE THE CHILDREN OF THE HIGHER MAN.

SO, AFRICA, UNITE.
AFRICA, UNITE.
UNITE FOR THE BENEFIT OF YOUR PEOPLE.
UNITE, FOR IT'S LATER THAN YOU THINK.

UNITE FOR THE BENEFIT OF YOUR CHILDREN.
UNITE, FOR IT'S LATER THAN YOU THINK.
AFRICA AWAITS ITS CREATORS,
AFRICA AWAITING ITS CREATORS.
AFRICA, YOU'RE MY FOREFATHER CORNERSTONE.
UNITE FOR THE AFRICANS ABROAD.
UNITE FOR THE AFRICANS A YARD.
AFRICA, UNITE.

AFRICA UNITE

Words and Music by Bob Marley

BELLY FULL
A.K.A. THEM BELLY FULL (BUT WE HUNGRY)
Words and Music by Bob Marley

NA-NA-NA-NA-NA-NA-NA-NA-NA;
NA-NA-NA-NA-NA-NA-NA-NA-NA;
NA-NA-NA-NA-NA-NA-NA-NA-NA;
NA-NA-NA-NA-NA-NA-NA-NA-NA.

THEM BELLY FULL BUT WE HUNGRY.
A HUNGRY MOB IS A ANGRY MOB.
A RAIN A-FALL BUT THE DIRT IT TOUGH;
A POT A-COOK BUT THE FOOD NO 'NOUGH.
YOU'RE GONNA DANCE TO JAH MUSIC, DANCE.
WE'RE GONNA DANCE TO JAH MUSIC, DANCE.
FORGET YOUR TROUBLES AND DANCE.
FORGET YOUR SORROW AND DANCE.
FORGET YOUR SICKNESS AND DANCE.
FORGET YOUR WEAKNESS AND DANCE.
COST OF LIVING GET SO HIGH,
RICH AND POOR, THEY START A CRY.
NOW THE WEAK MUST GET STRONG.
THEY SAY, "OH, WHAT A TRIBULATION."

THEM BELLY FULL BUT WE HUNGRY.
A HUNGRY MOB IS A ANGRY MOB.
A RAIN A-FALL BUT THE DIRT IT TOUGH;
A POT A-COOK BUT THE FOOD NO 'NOUGH.
WE'RE GONNA CHUCK TO JAH MUSIC,
    CHUCKIN'.
WE'RE CHUCKIN' TO JAH MUSIC,
    WE'RE CHUCKIN'.

A BELLY FULL BUT THEM HUNGRY.
A ANGRY MOB IS A ANGRY MOB.
A RAIN A-FALL BUT THE DIRT IT TOUGH;
A POT A-COOK BUT THE FOOD NO 'NOUGH.

A ANGRY MAN IS A ANGRY MAN.
A RAIN A-FALL BUT THE DIRT IT TOUGH;
A POT A-COOK BUT THE FOOD NO 'NOUGH.
(*REPEAT*)
A ANGRY MOB IS A ANGRY MOB.

BELLY FULL
A.K.A. THEM BELLY FULL (BUT WE HUNGRY)
Words and Music by Bob Marley

19

CONCRETE JUNGLE

Words and Music by Bob Marley

No sun will shine in my day today.
(No sun will shine.)
The high yellow moon won't come out to play.
(Won't come out to play.)
Darkness has covered my light (and has changed,)
And has changed my day into night.
Now where is this love to be found, won't someone tell me?
'Cause life, sweet life, must be somewhere to be found, yeah.
Instead of a concrete jungle where the livin' is hardest.
Concrete jungle, oh man, you've got to do your best, yeah.

No chains around my feet, but I'm not free.
I know I am bound here in captivity.
And I've never known happiness, and I've never known sweet caresses.
Still, I be always laughing like a clown.
Won't someone help me?
Cause, sweet life, I've, I've got to pick myself from off the ground, yeah,
    in this here concrete jungle,
I say, what do you got for me now?
Concrete jungle, oh, why won't you let me be now?

(Solo)

I said life must be somewhere to be found, yeah.
Instead of a concrete jungle, illusion, confusion.
Concrete jungle, yeah.
Concrete jungle, you name it, we got it, concrete jungle now.

Concrete jungle, what do you got for me now?

CONCRETE JUNGLE

Words and Music by Bob Marley

COMING IN FROM THE COLD

Words and Music by Bob Marley

IN THIS LIFE, IN THIS LIFE,
IN THIS LIFE, IN THIS OH SWEET LIFE
WE'RE COMING IN FROM THE COLD.
WE'RE COMING IN, COMING IN,
COMING IN, COMING IN,
COMING IN, COMING IN,
COMING IN FROM THE COLD.

IT'S YOU, IT'S YOU, IT'S YOU I'M TALKIN' TO.
WELL, IT'S YOU, YOU, YOU I'M TALKING TO NOW.
WHY DO YOU LOOK SO SAD AND FORSAKEN?
WHEN ONE DOOR IS CLOSED, DON'T YOU KNOW
    ANOTHER IS OPENED?

WOULD YOU LET THE SYSTEM MAKE YOU KILL
    YOUR BROTHER MAN? NO, DREAD, NO!
WOULD YOU MAKE THE SYSTEM MAKE YOU KILL
    YOUR BROTHER MAN? NO, DREAD, NO!
WOULD YOU MAKE THE SYSTEM GET ON TOP OF
    YOUR HEAD AGAIN? NO, DREAD, NO!
WELL, THE BIGGEST MAN YOU EVER DID SEE WAS,
    WAS JUST A BABY.

IN THIS LIFE, IN THIS LIFE, IN THIS,
IN THIS LIFE, OH SWEET LIFE
COMING IN FROM THE COLD.
WE'RE COMING IN, COMING IN,
COMING IN, COMING IN,
COMING IN, WOO,
COMING IN FROM THE COLD.
IT'S LIFE, IT'S LIFE, IT'S LIFE, IT'S LIFE,
IT'S LIFE, IT'S LIFE, IT'S WOAH, WELL,
COMING IN FROM THE COLD.

WE'RE COMING IN, COMING IN,
COMING IN, COMING, WOO,
COMING IN, COMING IN,
COMING IN FROM THE COLD.

IT'S YOU, IT'S YOU, IT'S YOU I'M TALKIN' TO.
WELL, IT'S YOU, YOU, YOU I'M TALKING TO NOW.
WHY DO YOU LOOK SO SAD AND FORSAKEN?
WHEN ONE DOOR IS CLOSED,
WHEN ONE DOOR IS CLOSED, MANY MORE IS OPENED.

WOULD YOU LET THE SYSTEM GET ON TOP OF
    YOUR HEAD AGAIN? NO, DREAD, NO!
WOULD YOU LET THE SYSTEM MAKE YOU KILL
    YOUR BROTHER MAN? NO, DREAD, NO!

WOULD YOU MAKE THE SYSTEM GET ON TOP OF
    YOUR HEAD AGAIN? NO, DREAD, NO!
WELL, THE BIGGEST MAN YOU EVER DID SEE
    WAS, WAS ONCE A BABY.

IN THIS LIFE, IN THIS LIFE, IN THIS,
IN THIS LIFE, OH SWEET LIFE
WE'RE COMING IN FROM THE COLD.
WE'RE COMING IN, WE'RE COMING IN,
COMING IN, COMING IN,
COMING IN, WOO,
COMING IN FROM THE COLD.
WE'RE COMING IN, COMING IN,
COMING IN, COMING IN, WHOA, YEAH,
COMING IN FROM THE COLD.
(*REPEAT*)

COMING IN FROM THE COLD

Words and Music by Bob Marley

COULD YOU BE LOVED

Words and Music by Bob Marley

COULD YOU BE LOVED AND BE LOVED? (*REPEAT*)

DON'T LET THEM FOOL YOU
    OR EVEN TRY TO SCHOOL YOU, OH, NO.
WE'VE GOT A MIND OF OUR OWN.
SO, GO TO HELL IF WHAT YOU'RE THINKIN' ISN'T RIGHT.
LOVE WOULD NEVER LEAVE US ALONE;
IN THE DARKNESS THERE MUST COME OUT TO LIGHT.

COULD YOU BE LOVED AND BE LOVED? (*REPEAT*)

THE ROAD OF LIFE IS ROCKY,
    AND YOU MAY STUMBLE, TOO.
SO WHILE YOU POINT YOUR FINGERS,
    SOMEONE ELSE IS JUDGIN' YOU.
LOVE YOUR BROTHER MAN.

COULD YOU BE, COULD YOU BE, COULD YOU BE LOVED?
COULD YOU BE, COULD YOU BE LOVED?

DON'T LET THEM CHANGE YOU,
    OR EVEN REARRANGE YOU. OH, NO.
WE'VE GOT A LIFE TO LIVE. OOH, OOH, OOH.
THEY SAY ONLY, ONLY,
    ONLY THE FITTEST OF THE FITTEST SHALL SURVIVE.
STAY ALIVE.

COULD YOU BE LOVED AND BE LOVED? (*REPEAT*)

YOU AIN'T GONNA MISS YOUR WATER
    UNTIL YOUR WELL RUNS DRY.
NO MATTER HOW YOU TREAT HIM,
    THE MAN WILL NEVER BE SATISFIED.

COULD YOU BE, COULD YOU BE, COULD YOU BE LOVED?
COULD YOU BE, COULD YOU BE LOVED?
(*REPEAT*)

SAY SOMETHIN', SAY SOMETHIN'. (*REPEAT*)

Could You Be Loved

Words and Music by Bob Marley

D.S. al Coda

EXODUS

Words and Music by Bob Marley

EXODUS, MOVEMENT OF JAH PEOPLE, OH YEAH.
OPEN YOUR EYES AND LET ME TELL YOU THIS.

MEN AND PEOPLE WILL FIGHT YA DOWN (TELL ME WHY?)
    WHEN YA SEE JAH LIGHT.
LET ME TELL YOU, IF YOU'RE NOT WRONG (THEN WHY?)
    EV'RYTHING IS ALRIGHT.
SO WE GONNA WALK, ALRIGHT,
    THROUGH THE ROADS OF CREATION.
WE'RE THE GENERATION (WELL ME WHY.)
    TROD THROUGH GREAT TRIBULATION.

EXODUS, MOVEMENT OF JAH PEOPLE.
EXODUS, MOVEMENT OF JAH PEOPLE.

OPEN YOUR EYES AND LOOK WITHIN.
ARE YOU SATISFIED WITH THE LIFE YOU'RE LIVING?
WE KNOW WHERE WE'RE GOING; WE KNOW WHERE WE'RE FROM.
WE'RE LEAVING BABYLON, WE'RE GOING TO OUR FATHERLAND.

EXODUS, MOVEMENT OF JAH PEOPLE.
 (MOVEMENT OF JAH PEOPLE.)
SEND US ANOTHER BROTHER MOSES GONNA CROSS THE RED SEA.
(MOVEMENT OF JAH PEOPLE.)
SEND US ANOTHER BROTHER MOSES GONNA CROSS THE RED SEA.

EXODUS, MOVEMENT OF JAH PEOPLE.
EXODUS, EXODUS, EXODUS, EXODUS,
EXODUS, EXODUS, EXODUS, EXODUS.
MOVE! MOVE! MOVE! MOVE! MOVE! MOVE!

OPEN YOUR EYES AND LOOK WITHIN.
ARE YOU SATISFIED WITH THE LIFE YOU'RE LIVING?
WE KNOW WHERE WE'RE GOING; WE KNOW WHERE WE'RE FROM.
WE'RE LEAVING BABYLON, WE'RE GOING TO THE FATHERLAND.

EXODUS, MOVEMENT OF JAH PEOPLE.
EXODUS, MOVEMENT OF JAH PEOPLE.
MOVEMENT OF JAH PEOPLE. (*4 TIMES*)
MOVE! MOVE! MOVE! MOVE! MOVE! MOVE! MOVE!

JAH COME TO BREAK DOWN 'PRESSION, RULE EQUALITY,
WIPE AWAY TRANSGRESSION, SET THE CAPTIVES FREE.

EXODUS, MOVEMENT OF JAH PEOPLE.
EXODUS, MOVEMENT OF JAH PEOPLE.
MOVEMENT OF JAH PEOPLE. (*5 TIMES*)

MOVE! MOVE! MOVE! MOVE! MOVE! MOVE!
MOVEMENT OF JAH PEOPLE. (*5 TIMES*)

Exodus

Words and Music by Bob Marley

44

move - ment of Jah peo - ple.

1,4

2

D.S.

3

(Move - ment of Jah peo - ple.)

Send us an - oth - er Broth-er

47

48

CODA

Move - ment of Jah peo -

- ple; move - ment of Jah peo - ple.

Jah come to break down 'pres - sion, rule e - qual - i - ty,

wipe a - way trans - gres - sion,

50

EASY SKANKING

Words and Music by Bob Marley

Easy skanking, skanking it easy.
Easy skanking, skanking it slow.
(REPEAT)

Excuse me while I light my spliff.
Oh God, I've got to take a lift.
From reality I just can't drift.
That's why I'm stayin' with this riff.

Take it easy. Lord, now take it easy.
Take it easy. Got to take it easy.
See, we're takin' it easy. We're taking' it slow.
We're takin' it easy. Got to take it slow.
So, take it easy. Oh, take it easy.
Take it easy. Take it easy.

Excuse me while I light my spliff.
Oh God, I've got to take a lift
From reality I just can't drift.
That's why I'm stayin' with this riff.

Take it easy. Got to take it easy.
Take it easy. Skanking, taking it slow.
Tell you what.
Herb for my wine;
    honey for my strong drink;
Herb for my wine;
    honey for my strong drink.

Take it easy. Skanking, take it easy.
Take it easy. Take it easy.
Takin' it easy. Skanking it slow.
Takin' it easy. Skanking it slow.

EASY SKANKING

Words and Music by Bob Marley

GET UP, STAND UP

Words and Music by Bob Marley

Get up, stand up, stand up for your right. *(3 times)*
Get up, stand up, don't give up the fight.

Preacher man, don't tell me heaven is under the earth.
I know you don't know what life is really worth.
Is not all that glitters is gold and, half the story has never been told.
So now you see the light, aay.
Stand up for your right. Come on.

Get up, stand up, stand up for your right.
Get up, stand up, don't give up the fight.
(Repeat)

Most people think great God will come from the sky,
Take away ev'rything, and make ev'rybody feel high.
But if you know what life is worth,
You would look for yours on earth.
And now you see the light.
You stand up for your right, yah!

Get up, stand up, stand up for your right.
Get up, stand up, don't give up the fight.
Get up, stand up. Life is your right,
So we can't give up the fight.
Stand up for you right, Lord, Lord.
Get up, stand up. Keep on struggling on,
Don't give up the fight.

We're sick and tired of your ism and skism game.
Die and go to heaven in Jesus' name, Lord.
We know when we understand.
Almighty God is a living man.
You can fool some people sometimes,
But you can't fool all the people all the time.
So now we see the light.
We gonna stand up for our right.

So you'd better get up, stand up, stand up for your right.
Get up, stand up, don't give up the fight.
Get up, stand up, stand up for your right.
Get up, stand up, don't give up the fight.

GET UP, STAND UP

Words and Music by Bob Marley

Get up,   stand up,   don't give up __ the fight.
Get up,   stand up,   don't give up __ the fight.
Get up,   stand up,   don't give up __ the fight.   We're

Preach-er man, don't tell __ me __   hea - ven is un - der the earth. __
Most peo - ple   think _   great God will come _ from the sky, __
sick and tired of your is - m and skism game. Die and go to hea-ven in Je - sus' name, Lord.

I know you don't _ know   what _ life is real - ly worth. _   Is not all __
take a - way ev - 'ry-thing,   and make ev -'ry-bod - y feel high.   But
We know when we un - der - stand.   Al -might - y God is a   liv -ing man. _ You can fool _

GUAVA JELLY

Words and Music by Bob Marley

YOU SAID YOU LOVE ME.
I SAID I LOVE YOU.
WHY WON'T YOU STOP YOUR CRYING?
DRY YOUR WEEPING EYES.
YOU KNOW THAT I LOVE,
I LOVE, I LOVE, I LOVE YOU SO, DAMSEL.
HERE I AM.
ME SAID, "COME RUB IT 'PON ME BELLY
    WITH YOU GUAVA JELLY, DAMSEL."
SAID, "HERE I STAND.
COME RUB IT 'PON ME BELLY WITH YOU GUAVA JELLY."
I REALLY, REALLY, I REALLY LOVE YOU.
YES, I REALLY, REALLY LOVE YOU, CHILD.

I'LL SAY YOU SHOULD STOP, STOP CRYING.
WIPE YOUR WEEPING EYES.
BABY, HOW I'M GONNA LOVE,
LOVE YOU FROM THE BOTTOM OF MY HEART.
DAMSEL, HERE I AM.
OH DAMSEL, COME RUB IT 'PON ME BELLY
    WITH YOUR GUAVA JELLY.
DAMSEL, HERE I STAND.
I CAN'T EXPLAIN, THOUGH THE FACT STILL REMAIN.
COME RUB IT 'PON ME BELLY WITH YOU GUAVA JELLY.
I NEED YOUR LOVE SO MUCH.
COME-A, COME-A, COME-A, COME-A,
    DAMSEL, OH DARLING.
OH, DAMSEL BABY, ME SAY COME RUB IT.
HERE I AM.
COME RUB IT 'PON ME BELLY WITH YOU GUAVA JELLY.

GUAVA JELLY

Words and Music by Bob Marley

I SHOT THE SHERIFF

Words and Music by Bob Marley

I SHOT THE SHERIFF, BUT I DIDN'T SHOOT NO DEPUTY.
   OH, NO, OH.
I SHOT THE SHERIFF, BUT I DIDN'T SHOOT NO DEPUTY.
   OOH, OOH, OOH. YEAH.

ALL AROUND IN MY HOMETOWN
THEY'RE TRYIN' TO TRACK ME DOWN, YEAH.
THEY SAY THEY WANT TO BRING ME IN GUILTY
FOR THE KILLING OF A DEPUTY,
   FOR THE LIFE OF A DEPUTY.
BUT I SAY, OH, NOW, NOW...

OH, I SHOT THE SHERIFF, BUT I SWEAR
   IT WAS IN SELF DEFENSE. OOH, OOH, OOH.
I SAID, I SHOT THE SHERIFF, OH LORD,
AND THEY SAY IT IS A CAPITAL OFFENSE.
   OOH, OOH, OOH. HEAR THIS.

SHERIFF JOHN BROWN ALWAYS HATED ME;
FOR WHAT, I DON'T KNOW.
EV'RY TIME I PLANT A SEED,
HE SAID, "KILL IT BEFORE IT GROWS."
HE SAID, "KILL THEM BEFORE THEY GROW."
AND SO, OH, NOW, NOW,
READ IT IN THE NEWS.

I SHOT THE SHERIFF, BUT I SWEAR IT WAS IN SELF DEFENSE.
   OOH, OOH, OOH. WHERE WAS THE DEPUTY?
I SAID, I SHOT THE SHERIFF, BUT I SWEAR
   IT WAS IN SELF DEFENSE.

FREEDOM CAME MY WAY ONE DAY,
AND I STARTED OUT OF TOWN, YEAH!
ALL OF A SUDDEN I SAW SHERIFF JOHN BROWN
AIMING TO SHOOT ME DOWN.
SO I SHOT, I SHOT, I SHOT HIM DOWN.
AND I SAY, IF I AM GUILTY I WILL PAY.

I SHOT THE SHERIFF, BUT I SAY, BUT I DIDN'T SHOOT NO DEPUTY.
   OH, NO, OH.
I SHOT THE SHERIFF, BUT I DIDN'T SHOOT NO DEPUTY.
   OOO, OOO, OOH.

REFLEXES HAD THE BETTER OF ME.
AND WHAT IS TO BE MUST BE.
EV'RY DAY THE BUCKET A-GO-A WELL;
ONE DAY THE BOTTOM A-GO DROP OUT.
ONE DAY THE BOTTOM A-GO DROP OUT.
I SAY, I, I, ...

I, I SHOT THE SHERIFF, BUT I DIDN'T SHOOT THE DEPUTY, NO.
(*REPEAT*)

I Shot The Sheriff

Words and Music by Bob Marley

66

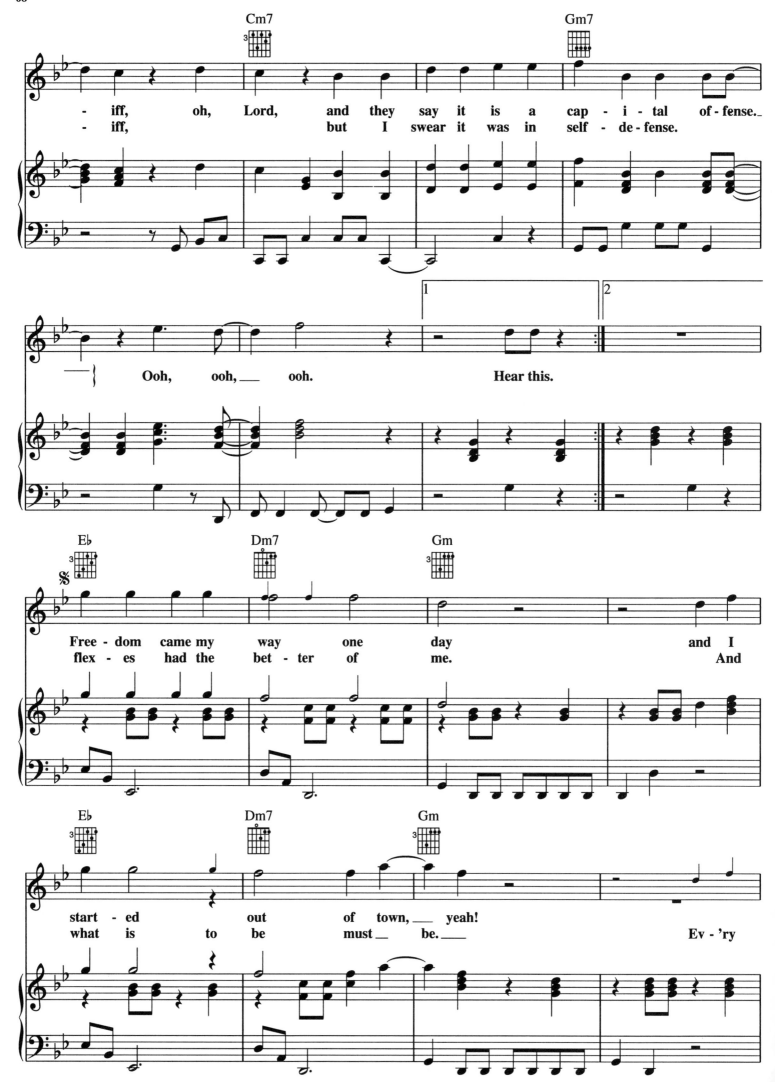

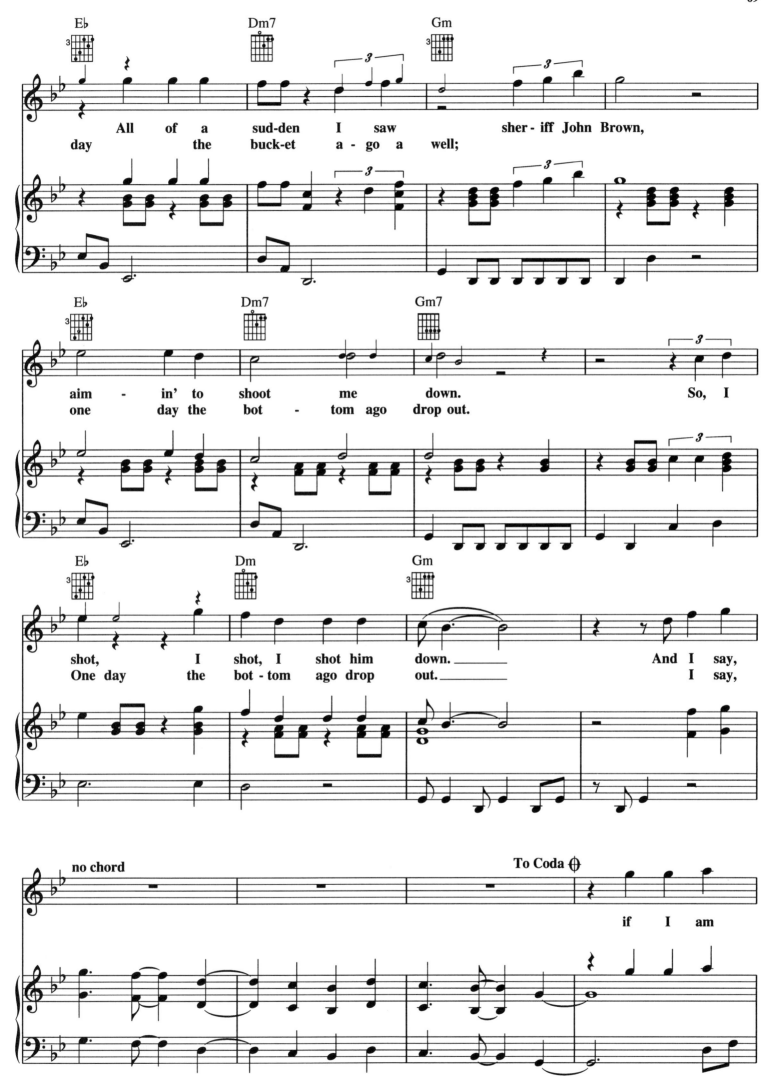

I'M HURTING INSIDE
a.k.a. HURTING INSIDE
Words and Music by Bob Marley

WHEN I WAS JUST A LITTLE CHILD,
HAPPINESS WAS THERE AWHILE.
THEN FROM ME, YEAH, IT SLIPPED ONE DAY.
HAPPINESS, COME BACK, I SAY.
'CAUSE IF YOU DON'T COME, I'VE GOT TO GO
    LOOKIN' FOR HAPPINESS.
WELL, IF YOU DON'T COME, I'VE GOT TO GO
    LOOKIN', LORD, FOR HAPPINESS, HAPPINESS.

I'M HURTING INSIDE.
I'M HURTING INSIDE.
OH, HEAR MY CRY, HEAR MY CRY, YEAH,
MY, MY, MY, MY, MY, MY, MY, MY CRY.

BEEN TOGETHER LIKE SCHOOL CHILDREN,
THEN YOU HURT ME JUST IN VAIN.
LORD, I'M YOUR WEARY CHILD.
HAPPINESS, COME BACK AWHILE.
'CAUSE IF YOU DON'T COME, I'VE GOT TO GO
    LOOKIN' FOR HAPPINESS.
THE ROAD IS DANGEROUS.
WELL, IF YOU DON'T COME, I'VE GOT TO GO
    LOOKIN', LORD, FOR HAPPINESS, HAPPINESS.
I'M HURTING INSIDE.
I'M HURTING INSIDE.

I'M HURTING INSIDE.
I'M HURTING INSIDE. (*REPEAT*)

FEEL THE PAIN, FEEL THE PAIN.
I'M HURTING INSIDE.
I'M HURTING INSIDE.

I'm Hurting Inside
a.k.a. Hurting Inside

Words and Music by Bob Marley

I'M STILL WAITING

Words and Music by Bob Marley

I'M STILL WAITING, I'M STILL WAITING,
I'M STILL WAITING, I'M STILL WAITING FOR YOU,
WHY OH WHY, WHY OH WHY?

I SAID MY FEET WON'T KEEP ME UP ANYMORE.
EV'RY LITTLE BEAT MY HEART BEATS, GIRL,
    IT'S AT YOUR DOOR.
I JUST WANNA LOVE YOU
AND I'M NEVER GONNA HURT YOU, GIRL.
SO WHY WON'T YOU COME OUT TO ME NOW, GIRL?
OH, CAN'T YOU SEE I'M UNDER YOUR SPELL?
BUT, I GOT TO, GOT TO GO.

WHY, GIRL, OH WHY, GIRL?

WHOA, MY GOSH THE RAIN IS FALLING,
AND I JUST CAN'T STOP CALLING.
AND I JUST CAN'T TELL THE RAINDROPS
    FROM MY TEARDROPS
FALLING DOWN MY FACE.
LOOK AT IT,
IT ISN'T REALLY RAINDROPS.

I'M STILL WAITING,
TEARDROPS FALLING DOWN MY FACE.
I'M STILL WAITING, I'M STILL WAITING,
I'M STILL WAITING, I'M STILL WAITING,
    YES I WILL.

I WAIT IN THE RAIN, I WAIT IN THE SUN.
PLEASE, RELIEVE ME FROM THESE PAINS,
    OH PAINS, JUST PAINS.
I LOVE YOU, YES I DO.
BUT TELL ME, DO YOU REALLY LOVE ME, TOO.

I'm Still Waiting

Words and Music by Bob Marley

IS THIS LOVE

Words and Music by Bob Marley

I WANNA LOVE YOU, AND TREAT YOU RIGHT.
I WANNA LOVE YOU, EVERY DAY AND EVERY NIGHT.
WE'LL BE TOGETHER, WITH A ROOF RIGHT OVER OUR HEADS.
WE'LL SHARE THE SHELTER OF MY SINGLE BED.
WE'LL SHARE THE SAME ROOM, JAH PROVIDE THE BREAD.

IS THIS LOVE, IS THIS LOVE,
IS THIS LOVE, IS THIS LOVE THAT I'M FEELIN'?
(*REPEAT*)

I WANNA KNOW, WANNA KNOW, WANNA KNOW NOW.
I GOT TO KNOW, GOT TO KNOW, GOT TO KNOW NOW.

I, I'M WILLING AND ABLE,
SO I THROW MY CARDS ON YOUR TABLE.
I WANNA LOVE YOU;
I WANNA LOVE YOU AND TREAT YOU RIGHT.
I WANNA LOVE YOU, EVERY DAY AND EVERY NIGHT.
WE'LL BE TOGETHER, WITH A ROOF RIGHT OVER OUR HEADS.
WE'LL SHARE THE SHELTER OF MY SINGLE BED.
WE'LL SHARE THE SAME ROOM, OH, JAH PROVIDE THE BREAD.

IS THIS LOVE, IS THIS LOVE,
IS THIS LOVE, IS THIS LOVE THAT I'M FEELIN'?
(*REPEAT*)

OH, YES I KNOW, YES I KNOW, YES I KNOW NOW. (*REPEAT*)
I, I'M WILLING AND ABLE,
SO I THROW MY CARDS ON YOUR TABLE.
SEE, I WANNA LOVE YOU,
I WANNA LOVE AND TREAT YOU RIGHT,
   LOVE AND TREAT YOU RIGHT.
I WANNA LOVE YOU EVERY DAY AND EVERY NIGHT.
WE'LL BE TOGETHER WITH A ROOF RIGHT OVER OUR HEADS.
WE'LL SHARE THE SHELTER OF MY SINGLE BED.
WE'LL SHARE THE SAME ROOM, JAH PROVIDE THE BREAD.
WE'LL SHARE THE SHELTER OF MY SINGLE BED.

Is This Love

Words and Music by Bob Marley

Iron Lion Zion

Words and Music by Bob Marley

I'M ON THE ROCK
AND THEN I CHECK A STOCK.
I HAD TO RUN LIKE A FUGITIVE
TO SAVE THE LIFE I LIVE.

I'M GONNA BE IRON, LIKE A LION, IN ZION.
I'M GONNA BE IRON, LIKE A LION, IN ZION,
   OHH YEAH.
LION, IRON, ZION, LION, ZION.

I'M ON THE RUN
BUT I AIN'T GOT NO GUN.
SEE, THEY WANT TO BE THE STAR,
SO THEY FIGHTING TRIBAL WAR.
AND THEY SAYING,

IRON LIKE A LION IN ZION;
IRON LIKE A LION IN ZION,
   IRON, LION, ZION.

I'M ON THE ROCK, I CHECK A STOCK.
I HAD TO RUN LIKE A FUGITIVE, OHH GOD.
JUST, JUST TO SAVE THE LIFE I LIVE, OHH NOW.
AND STILL I'M GONNA BE

IRON LIKE A LION IN ZION (WHAT DID I SAY?)
I'M GONNA BE IRON, LIKE A LION IN ZION.
WHAT DID YOU SAY, IRON, LION, ZION.

I'M ON THE RUN
BUT I DON'T GOT NO GUN.
SEE, MY BROTHERS WANNA BE THE STARS,
SO THEY ARE FIGHTING TRIBAL WARS.
AND THEY SAYING,

IRON LIKE A LION IN ZION.
IRON LIKE A LION IN ZION.
IRON, LION, ZION.
I'M ON A RUN, GOT NO GUN,
IRON, LION, ZION.

Iron Lion Zion

Words and Music by Bob Marley

I check a stock.

I had to run like a fug - i - tive

just

to, just to save the life____ I live,____ oh now.

JAMMIN'

Words and Music by Bob Marley

OOH, YEAH; WELL, ALRIGHT.
WE'RE JAMMIN'.
I WANNA JAM IT WITH YOU.
WE'RE JAMMIN', JAMMIN',
AND I HOPE YOU LIKE JAMMIN', TOO.
AIN'T NO RULES, AIN'T NO VOW,
WE CAN DO IT ANYHOW.
I AND I WILL SEE YOU THROUGH.
'CAUSE EVERY DAY WE PAY THE PRICE.
WE ARE THE LIVING SACRIFICE,
JAMMIN' TILL THE JAM IS THROUGH.

WE'RE JAMMIN'.
TO THINK THAT JAMMIN' WAS A THING OF THE PAST.
WE'RE JAMMIN',
AND I HOPE THIS JAM IS GONNA LAST.
NO BULLET CAN STOP US NOW,
WE NEITHER BEG NOR WE WON'T BOW.
NEITHER CAN BE BOUGHT NOR SOLD.
WE ALL DEFEND THE RIGHT,
JAH JAH CHILDREN MUST UNITE,
FOR LIFE IS WORTH MUCH MORE THAN GOLD.

WE'RE JAMMIN', JAMMIN', JAMMIN', JAMMIN'.
AND WE'RE JAMMIN' IN THE NAME OF THE LORD.
WE'RE JAMMIN', JAMMIN', JAMMIN', JAMMIN'.
WE'RE JAMMIN' RIGHT STRAIGHT FROM YARD.
SINGING HOLY MOUNT ZION, HOLY MOUNT ZION.
JAH SITTETH IN MOUNT ZION AND RULES ALL CREATION.
YEAH, WE'RE JAMMIN'. BOP-CHU-WA-WA-WA.

WE'RE JAMMIN'.
I WANNA JAM IT WITH YOU.
WE'RE JAMMIN', JAMMIN', JAMMIN', JAMMIN'.
AND JAMDOWN HOPE YOU'RE JAMMIN', TOO.
JAH KNOWS HOW MUCH I 'AVE TRIED.
THE TRUTH CANNOT HIDE
TO KEEP YOU SATISFIED.
TRUE LOVE THAT NOW EXISTS
IS THE LOVE I CAN'T RESIST,
SO JAM BY MY SIDE.

WE'RE JAMMIN', JAMMIN', JAMMIN', JAMMIN'.
I WANNA JAM IT WITH YOU.
WE'RE JAMMIN', WE'RE JAMMIN', WE'RE JAMMIN', WE'RE JAMMIN',
WE'RE JAMMIN', WE'RE JAMMIN', WE'RE JAMMIN', WE'RE JAMMIN'.
HOPE YOU LIKE JAMMIN', TOO.
(*REPEAT*)

Jammin'

Words and Music by Bob Marley

LIVELY UP YOURSELF

Words and Music by Bob Marley

YOU'RE GONNA LIVELY UP YOURSELF AND
 DON'T BE NO DRAG;
YOU LIVELY UP YOURSELF, OH
 REGGAE IS ANOTHER BAG.
YOU LIVELY UP YOURSELF AND DON'T SAY NO.
YOU'RE GONNA LIVELY UP YOURSELF
 'CAUSE I SAID SO.
(HEAR WHAT YOU GONNA DO.)
YOU ROCK SO, YOU ROCK SO,
LIKE YOU NEVER DID BEFORE.
YOU DIP SO, YOU DIP SO,
DIP THRU MY DOOR.
YOU COME SO, YOU COME SO,
 OH, YEAH.
YOU SKANK SO, YOU SKANK SO,
 BE ALIVE TODAY.

YOU'RE GONNA LIVELY UP YOURSELF AND
 DON'T SAY NO.
YOU LIVELY UP YOURSELF,
 BIG DADDY SAYS SO.
YOU LIVELY UP YOURSELF AND
 DON'T BE NO DRAG.
YOU LIVELY UP YOURSELF
 'CAUSE REGGAE IS ANOTHER BAG.

WHAT YOU GOT THAT I DON'T KNOW?
I'M A-TRYING TO WONDER WHY YOU ACT SO.
(HEY, DO YOU HEAR WHAT THE MAN SEH?)
LIVELY UP YOUR WOMAN IN THE
 MORNING TIME, YOU'ALL,
KEEP A LIVELY UP YOUR WOMAN WHEN
 THE EVENING COME AND TAKE HER, TAKE YA.

YOU ROCK SO, YOU ROCK SO,
YOU DIP SO, YOU DIP SO,
YOU SKANK SO, YOU SKANK SO,
 AND DON'T BE NO DRAG.
YOU COME SO, YOU COME SO,
 FOR REGGAE IS ANOTHER BAG.

GET WHAT YOU GOT IN THAT BAG.
WHAT HAVE YOU GOT IN THE OTHER BAG
 YOU GOT HANGING THERE?
WHAT YOU SAY YOU GOT?
I DON'T BELIEVE YOU!

LIVELY UP YOURSELF

Words and Music by Bob Marley

LICK SAMBA

Words and Music by Bob Marley

LICK SAMBA, LICK SAMBA, LICK SAMBA,
   OH, LICK SAMBA.
ME SAY, LICK SAMBA, LICK SAMBA.
   OH NOW, OH LICK SAMBA.

I COULD NOT RESIST, LICK SAMBA, LICK SAMBA,
OH NOW, ANOTHER LIKE THIS, LICK SAMBA.
OH NOW, OH LICK SAMBA.
AND THOUGH I KNOW YOU'LL HURT ME AGAIN,
   OH LICK SAMBA,
I'LL GO ON, I'LL FEEL THE PAIN,
   OH LICK SAMBA.
AND IT'S NOT THAT I AM WEAK,
   OH LICK SAMBA.
BUT IT'S THAT I'M ON A PEAK, OH DARLING,

OH LICK SAMBA. JUST A...

LICK SAMBA, LICK SAMBA, LICK SAMBA.
I SAY, OH LICK SAMBA.
OH NOW, OH LICK SAMBA, OH LICK SAMBA.

BRING IT UP A-LICK IT ONE TIME,
   OH LICK SAMBA.
I'LL SETTLE THE LITTLE A CLAIM,
   OH LICK SAMBA.

YOU CAN WRITE IT DOWN IN MY NAME,
   OH LICK SAMBA.
MORNING TIME, NOON OR NIGHT,
   OH LICK SAMBA.

LICK SAMBA, LICK SAMBA, LICK SAMBA,
   OH LICK SAMBA.

LICK SAMBA, LICK SAMBA, LICK SAMBA,
OH LICK SAMBA, OH DARLING,
   OH LICK SAMBA.
IF IT'S MORNING TIME, I'M READY,
   OH LICK SAMBA.
AND IF IT'S LATE AT NIGHT, I'M STEADY,

Lick Samba

Words and Music by Bob Marley

NATURAL MYSTIC
Words and Music by Bob Marley

THERE'S A NAT'RAL MYSTIC BLOWING THROUGH THE AIR.
IF YOU LISTEN CAREFULLY NOW, YOU WILL HEAR.
THIS COULD BE THE FIRST TRUMPET,
    MIGHT AS WELL BE THE LAST.
MANY MORE WILL HAVE TO SUFFER,
    MANY MORE WILL HAVE TO DIE.
DON'T ASK ME WHY.
THINGS ARE NOT THE WAY THEY USED TO BE.
I WON'T TELL NO LIE.

ONE AND ALL GOT TO FACE REALITY NOW.
THOUGH I TRY TO FIND THE ANSWER
    TO ALL THE QUESTIONS THEY ASK,
THOUGH I KNOW IT'S IMPOSSIBLE
    TO GO LIVING THROUGH THE PAST.
DON'T TELL NO LIE.

THERE'S A NAT'RAL MYSTIC BLOWING THROUGH THE AIR.
CAN'T KEEP THEM DOWN.
IF YOU LISTEN CAREFULLY NOW, YOU WILL HEAR.
SUCH A NAT'RAL MYSTIC BLOWING THROUGH THE AIR.

THIS COULD BE THE FIRST TRUMPET,
    MIGHT AS WELL BE THE LAST.
MANY MORE WILL HAVE TO SUFFER,
    MANY MORE WILL HAVE TO DIE.
DON'T ASK ME WHY.

THERE'S A NAT'RAL MYSTIC BLOWING THROUGH THE AIR.
I WON'T TELL NO LIE.
IF YOU LISTEN CAREFULLY NOW, YOU WILL HEAR.
THERE'S A NAT'RAL MYSTIC BLOWING THROUGH THE AIR.
SUCH A NAT'RAL MYSTIC BLOWING THROUGH THE AIR.

THERE'S A NAT'RAL MYSTIC BLOWING THROUGH THE AIR.
SUCH A NAT'RAL MYSTIC BLOWING THROUGH THE AIR.
(*REPEAT*)

Natural Mystic

Words and Music by Bob Marley

NICE TIME

Words and Music by Bob Marley

LONG TIME WE NO HAVE NO NICE TIME,
DOO-YOO-DEE-DUN-DOO-YEA.
THINK ABOUT THAT.
(REPEAT)

THIS IS MY HEART TO ROCK YOU STEADY.
I'LL GIVE YOU LOVE THE TIME YOU'RE READY.
THIS LITTLE HEART IN ME
    JUST WON'T LET ME BE.
I'M JUST TO ROCK YOU, NOW.
WON'T YOU ROCK WITH ME?
LONG TIME WE NO HAVE NO NICE TIME,
DOO-YOO-DEE-DUN-DOO-YEA.
THINK ABOUT THAT.
(REPEAT)

Nice Time

Words and Music by Bob Marley

doo yoo - dee-dun - doo, yea. Think _ a-bout that.

MELLOW MOOD

Words and Music by Bob Marley

I'LL PLAY YOUR FAV'RITE SONG, DARLIN'.
WE CAN ROCK IT ALL NIGHT LONG, DARLIN'.
'CAUSE I'VE GOT LOVE, DARLIN',
LOVE, SWEET LOVE, DARLIN'.
MELLOW MOOD HAS GOT ME,
SO LET THE MUSIC ROCK ME.

'CAUSE I'VE GOT LOVE, DARLIN',
LOVE, SWEET LOVE, DARLIN'.
QUIET AS THE NIGHT,
PLEASE TURN OFF YOUR LIGHT.

I'LL PLAY YOUR FAV'RITE SONG, DARLIN'.
WE CAN ROCK IT ALL NIGHT LONG, DARLIN'.

STRIKE THE HAMMER WHILE IRON IS HOT.
STRIKE THE HAMMER WHILE IRON IS HOT.
STRIKE THE HAMMER WHILE IRON IS HOT.
OPEN UP YOUR HEART.
OPEN UP YOUR HEART.
LET LOVE COME RUNNING IN, DARLIN',
LOVE, SWEET LOVE, DARLIN'.
LOVE, SWEET LOVE, DARLIN'.

STRIKE THE HAMMER WHILE IRON IS HOT.
STRIKE THE HAMMER WHILE IRON IS HOT.
STRIKE THE HAMMER WHILE IRON IS HOT.
OPEN UP YOUR HEART.
OPEN UP YOUR HEART.
LET LOVE COME RUNNING IN, DARLIN',
LOVE, SWEET LOVE, DARLIN'.
LOVE, SWEET LOVE, DARLIN'.

MELLOW MOOD HAS GOT ME, DARLIN'.
LET THE MUSIC ROCK ME, DARLIN'.
'CAUSE I GOT YOUR LOVE, DARLIN'.
LOVE, SWEET LOVE, DARLIN'.

LOVE, SWEET LOVE, DARLIN'.
(*REPEAT*)

MELLOW MOOD

Words and Music by Bob Marley

NO WOMAN NO CRY

Words and Music by Vincent Ford

No WOMAN, NO CRY. (*4 TIMES*)

'CAUSE I REMEMBER WHEN WE USED TO SIT
IN THE GOVERNMENT YARD IN TRENCHTOWN.
OBA, OB-SERVING THE HYPOCRITES
AS THEY WOULD MINGLE WITH THE GOOD
PEOPLE WE MEET;
GOOD FRIENDS WE HAVE HAD, OH GOOD
   FRIENDS WE'VE LOST ALONG THE WAY.
IN THIS BRIGHT FUTURE YOU CAN'T FORGET
   YOUR PAST,
SO DRY YOUR TEARS, I SAY.

NO WOMAN, NO CRY.
NO WOMAN, NO CRY.
LITTLE DARLIN', DON'T SHED NO TEARS.
NO WOMAN, NO CRY.

SAID, SAID, SAID I REMEMBER WHEN WE USED
   TO SIT
IN THE GOVERNMENT YARD IN TRENCHTOWN.
AND THEN GEORGIE WOULD MAKE THE FIRE
   LIGHT,
LOG WOOD BURNIN' THROUGH THE NIGHT.

THEN WE WOULD COOK CORN MEAL PORRIDGE
OF WHICH I'LL SHARE WITH YOU.
MY FEET IS MY ONLY CARRIAGE,
SO I'VE GOT TO PUSH ON THROUGH,
BUT WHILE I'M GONE,...

EV'RYTHING'S GONNA BE ALRIGHT. (*7 TIMES*)
EV'RYTHING'S GONNA BE ALRIGHT,
SO, NO WOMAN, NO CRY.
NO, NO WOMAN, NO WOMAN, NO CRY.
OH, LITTLE DARLING, DON'T SHED NO TEARS.
NO WOMAN, NO CRY.

NO WOMAN, NO WOMAN, NO WOMAN, NO CRY.
NO WOMAN, NO CRY.
OH, MY LITTLE DARLIN', PLEASE DON'T SHED
   NO TEARS.
NO WOMAN, NO CRY, YEAH.

NO WOMAN, NO WOMAN, NO CRY.

No Woman No Cry

Words and Music by Vincent Ford

PLEASE DON'T
ROCK MY BOAT

Words and Music by Bob Marley

OH, PLEASE DON'T YOU ROCK MY BOAT
'CAUSE I DON'T WANT MY BOAT TO BE ROCKING.
DON'T ROCK MY BOAT. (*REPEAT*)

I'M TELLING YOU THAT, OH-WHOOH-WHOOH,
I LIKE IT LIKE THIS, I LIKE IT LIKE THIS.
AND YOU SHOULD KNOW, YOU SHOULD KNOW BY NOW
I LIKE IT, I LIKE IT LIKE THIS,
   I LIKE IT LIKE THIS.
YEAH ... SOUL, SATISFY MY SOUL.
   ... TISFY MY SOUL.
... E IS A REACTION.
... HAVE DONE FOR ME?
... THE TIME.

WHE...
I FEEL L... WINNER.
WHEN I MEE... UND THE CORNER,
YOU MAKE ME FEEL LIKE A
   SWEEP-STAKE WINNER.
WHOA CHILD, CAN'T YOU SEE,
   YOU MUST BELIEVE ME.
OH DARLING, DARLING, I'M CALLING, CALLING.
CAN'T YOU SEE, WHY WON'T YOU BELIEVE ME.
OH DARLING, DARLING, I'M CALLING, CALLING.

WHEN I MEET YOU AROUND THE CORNER,
OH, I SAID BABY, NEVER LET ME BE A LONER.
AND THEN YOU HOLD ME TIGHT,
   YOU MAKE ME FEEL ALRIGHT.
YES, WHEN YOU HOLD ME TIGHT,
   YOU MADE ME FEEL ALRIGHT.

WHOA, HONEY, CAN'T YOU SEE,
   DON'T YOU BELIEVE ME?
OH DARLING, DARLING, I'M CALLING, CALLING.
CAN'T YOU SEE, WHY WON'T YOU BELIEVE ME?
OH DARLING, DARLING, I'M CALLING, CALLING.

SATISFY MY SOUL, SATISFY MY SOUL,
   SATISFY MY SOUL.
THAT'S ALL I WANT FROM YOU,
   THAT'S ALL I'LL TAKE FROM YOU.
SATISFY MY SOUL, SATISFY MY SOUL.

PLEASE DON'T ROCK MY BOAT

Words and Music by Bob Marley

ONE LOVE

Words and Music by Bob Marley

ONE LOVE, ONE HEART.
LET'S GET TOGETHER AND FEEL ALL RIGHT.
HEAR THE CHILDREN CRYING. (ONE LOVE.)
HEAR THE CHILDREN CRYING. (ONE HEART.)
SAYIN', "GIVE THANKS AND PRAISE TO THE LORD
   AND I WILL FEEL ALL RIGHT."
SAYIN', "LET'S GET TOGETHER AND FEEL ALL RIGHT."
WHOA, WHOA, WHOA, WHOA.

LET THEM ALL PASS ALL THEIR DIRTY REMARKS.
   (ONE LOVE.)
THERE IS ONE QUESTION I'D REALLY LOVE TO ASK.
   (ONE HEART.)
IS THERE A PLACE FOR THE HOPELESS SINNER
WHO HAS HURT ALL MANKIND JUST TO SAVE HIS OWN?
BELIEVE ME.

ONE LOVE, ONE HEART.
LET'S GET TOGETHER AND FEEL ALL RIGHT.
AS IT WAS IN THE BEGINNING, (ONE LOVE.)
SO SHALL IT BE IN THE END. (ONE HEART.)
ALRIGHT, "GIVE THANKS AND PRAISE TO THE LORD
   AND I WILL FEEL ALL RIGHT."
"LET'S GET TOGETHER AND FEEL ALL RIGHT."
ONE MORE THING.

LET'S GET TOGETHER TO FIGHT THIS HOLY
   ARMAGEDDON, (ONE LOVE.)
SO WHEN THE MAN COMES THERE WILL BE NO,
   NO DOOM. (ONE SONG.)
HAVE PITY ON THOSE WHOSE CHANCES GROW THINNER.
THERE AIN'T NO HIDING PLACE FROM THE FATHER OF
   CREATION.

SAYIN', "ONE LOVE, ONE HEART.
LET'S GET TOGETHER AND FEEL ALL RIGHT."
I'M PLEADING TO MANKIND. (ONE LOVE.)
OH, LORD. (ONE HEART.) WHOA.

"GIVE THANKS AND PRAISE TO THE LORD
   AND I WILL FEEL ALL RIGHT."
LET'S GET TOGETHER AND FEEL ALL RIGHT.
(REPEAT)

One Love

Words and Music by Bob Marley

SMALL AXE

Words and Music by Bob Marley

WHY BOASTETH THYSELF, OH EVIL MEN,
PLAYING SMART AND NOT BEING CLEVER?
I SAY YOU'RE WORKING INIQUITY TO ACHIEVE
    VANITY, YEAH,
BUT THE GOODNESS OF JAH JAH ENDURETH
    FOREVER.

IF YOU ARE THE BIG TREE,
    WE ARE THE SMALL AXE
SHARPENED TO CUT YOU DOWN,
    READY TO CUT YOU DOWN.

THESE ARE THE WORDS OF MY MASTER.
KEEP ON TELLING ME
    NO WEAK HEART SHALL PROSPER,
OH, NO THEY CAN'T.

AND WHOSOEVER DIGGETH A PIT, LORD,
    SHALL FALL IN IT, SHALL FALL IN IT.
WHOSOEVER DIGGETH A PIT SHALL BURY IN IT,
    SHALL BURY IN IT.

IF YOU ARE THE BIG TREE, WE ARE THE SMALL AXE
SHARPENED TO CUT YOU DOWN, READY TO CUT YOU DOWN.

AND WHOSOEVER DIGGETH A PIT SHALL FALL IN IT,
    FALL IN IT.
WHOSOEVER DIGGETH A PIT SHALL BURY IN IT,
    SHALL BURY IN IT.

IF YOU HAVE A BIG TREE, WE HAVE A SMALL AXE
READY TO CUT YOU DOWN,
    SHARPENED TO CUT YOU DOWN.

IF YOU ARE THE BIG TREE, WE ARE THE SMALL AXE
READY TO CUT YOU DOWN, SHARPENED TO CUT YOU DOWN.

SMALL AXE

Words and Music by Bob Marley

REDEMPTION SONG

Words and Music by Bob Marley

OLD PIRATES, YES, THEY ROB I.
SOLD I TO THE MERCHANT SHIPS
    MINUTES AFTER THEY TOOK I FROM THE BOTTOMLESS PIT.
BUT MY HAND WAS MADE STRONG
    BY THE HAND OF THE ALMIGHTY.
WE FORWARD IN THIS GENERATION TRIUMPHANTLY.

CHORUS
WON'T YOU HELP TO SING THESE SONGS OF FREEDOM?
'CAUSE ALL I EVER HAD, REDEMPTION SONGS,
REDEMPTION SONGS.

EMANCIPATE YOURSELVES FROM MENTAL SLAVERY,
NONE BUT OURSELVES CAN FREE OUR MINDS.
HAVE NO FEAR FOR ATOMIC ENERGY,
'CAUSE NONE OF THEM CAN STOP THE TIME.
HOW LONG SHALL THEY KILL OUR PROPHETS
WHILE WE STAND ASIDE AND LOOK?
YES, SOME SAY IT'S JUST A PART OF IT.
WE'VE GOT TO FULFILL THE BOOK.
TO CHORUS

EMANCIPATE YOURSELVES FROM MENTAL SLAVERY,
NONE BUT OURSELVES CAN FREE OUR MINDS.
HAVE NO FEAR FOR ATOMIC ENERGY,
'CAUSE NONE OF THEM CAN STOP THE TIME.
HOW LONG SHALL THEY KILL OUR PROPHETS
WHILE WE STAND ASIDE AND LOOK?
YES, SOME SAY IT'S JUST A PART OF IT.
WE'VE GOT TO FULFILL THE BOOK.

WON'T YOU HELP TO SING THESE SONGS OF FREEDOM?
'CAUSE ALL I EVER HAD, REDEMPTION SONGS,
ALL I EVER HAD, REDEMPTION SONGS,
THESE SONGS OF FREEDOM, SONGS OF FREEDOM.

REDEMPTION SONG

Words and Music by Bob Marley

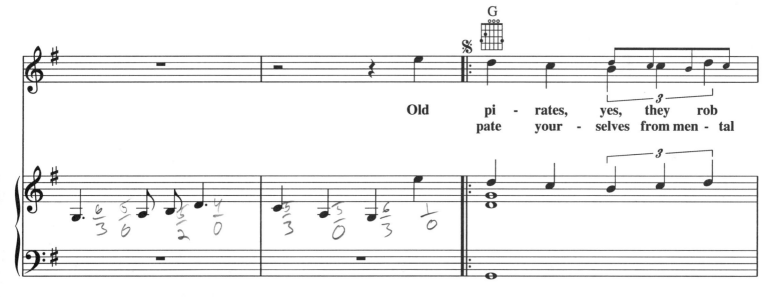

Old pi - rates, yes, they rob
pate your - selves from men - tal

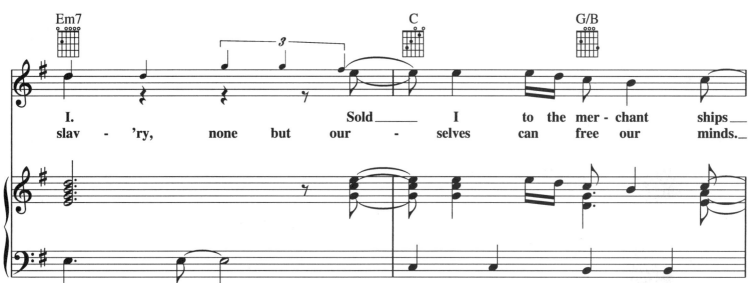

I. slav - 'ry, none but our - selves can free our minds.
Sold I to the mer - chant ships

SO MUCH TROUBLE IN THE WORLD

Words and Music by Bob Marley

SO MUCH TROUBLE IN THE WORLD.
SO MUCH TROUBLE IN THE WORLD.

BLESS MY EYES THIS MORNING,
JAH SUN IS ON THE RISE ONCE AGAIN.
THE WAY EARTHLY THINGS ARE GOING,
ANYTHING CAN HAPPEN.

YOU SEE MEN SAILING ON THEIR EGO TRIPS,
BLAST OFF ON THEIR SPACESHIPS,
    MILLION MILES FROM REALITY;
NO CARE FOR YOU, NO CARE FOR ME.

SO MUCH TROUBLE IN THE WORLD.
SO MUCH TROUBLE IN THE WORLD.
ALL YOU GOT TO DO IS
GIVE A LITTLE, TAKE A LITTLE,
GIVE A LITTLE, ONE MORE TIME.
GIVE A LITTLE, TAKE A LITTLE,
GIVE A LITTLE.

SO YOU THINK YOU FOUND THE SOLUTION,
BUT IT'S JUST ANOTHER ILLUSION.
SO BEFORE YOU CHECK OUT THIS TIDE
DON'T LEAVE ANOTHER CORNERSTONE
    STANDING THERE BEHIND.

WE'VE GOT TO FACE THE DAY,
OOH WEE, COME WHAT MAY.
WE THE STREET PEOPLE TALKING,
WE THE PEOPLE STRUGGLING.
NOW THEY'RE SITTING ON A TIME BOMB;
NOW I KNOW THE TIME HAS COME.
WHAT GOES ON UP IS COMING ON DOWN,
GOES AROUND AND COMES AROUND.

SO MUCH TROUBLE IN THE WORLD.
SO MUCH TROUBLE IN THE WORLD.

THERE IS SO MUCH TROUBLE IN THE WORLD.
SO MUCH TROUBLE IN THE WORLD.
(*REPEAT*)

So Much Trouble In The World

Words and Music by Bob Marley

SUN IS SHINING

Words and Music by Bob Marley

SUN IS SHINING, THE WEATHER IS SWEET.
MAKE YOU WANT TO MOVE YOUR DANCING FEET.
TO THE RESCUE, HERE I AM.
WANT YOU TO KNOW, Y'ALL, WHERE I STAND.

(MONDAY MORNING), HERE I AM.
WANT YOU TO KNOW JUST IF YOU CAN,
(TUESDAY EVENING) WHERE I STAND.
(WEDNESDAY MORNING),
   TELL MYSELF A NEW DAY IS RISING.
(THURSDAY EVENING), GET ON THE RISE,
   A NEW DAY IS DAWNING.
(FRIDAY MORNING), HERE I AM.
(SATURDAY EVENING), WANT YOU TO KNOW JUST,
WANT YOU TO KNOW JUST WHERE I STAND.

WHEN THE MORNING GATHERS THE RAINBOW,
WANT YOU TO KNOW I'M A RAINBOW, TOO.
SO, TO THE RESCUE, HERE I AM.
WANT YOU TO KNOW JUST IF YOU CAN,
WHERE I STAND, KNOW, KNOW, KNOW, KNOW, KNOW.

WE'LL LIFT OUR HEADS AND GIVE JAH PRAISES.
WE'LL LIFT OUR HEADS AND GIVE JAH PRAISES, YEAH.

SUN IS SHINING, THE WEATHER IS SWEET.
MAKE YOU WANT TO MOVE YOUR DANCING FEET.
TO THE RESCUE, HERE I AM.
WANT YOU TO KNOW JUST IF YOU CAN,
WHERE I STAND;
KNOW, KNOW, KNOW, KNOW WHERE I STAND.

MONDAY MORNING, SCOO-BE-DOOP-SCOOP SCOOP;
TUESDAY EVENING, SCOO-BE-DOOP-SCOOP-SCOOP;
WEDNESDAY MORNING, SCOO-BE-DOOP-SCOOP-SCOOP;
THURSDAY EVENING, SCOO-BE-DOOP-SCOOP-SCOOP;
FRIDAY MORNING, SCOO-BE-DOOP-SCOOP-SCOOP;
SATURDAY EVENING, SCOO-BE-DOOP-SCOOP-SCOOP.

SO TO THE RESCUE, TO THE RESCUE, TO THE RESCUE,
AWAKE FROM YOUR SLEEP AND SLUMBER.
TODAY COULD BRING YOUR LUCKY NUMBER.

SUN IS SHINING, THE WEATHER IS SWEET. (*REPEAT*)

Sun Is Shining

Words and Music by Bob Marley

SOUL REBEL
Words and Music by Bob Marley

I'M A REBEL, SOUL REBEL.
I'M A CAPTURER, SOUL ADVENTURER.
I'M A REBEL, SOUL REBEL.
I'M A CAPTURER, SOUL ADVENTURER.

SEE THE MORNING SUN, THE MORNING SUN,
   ON THE HILLSIDE.
IF YOU'RE NOT LIVING GOOD, TRAVEL WIDE,
   YOU GOTTA TRAVEL WIDE.
SAID I'M A LIVING MAN,
   AND I'VE GOT WORK TO DO.
IF YOU'RE NOT HAPPY, CHILDREN,
  THEN YOU MUST BE BLUE,
   MUST BE BLUE, PEOPLE SAY.

I'M A REBEL, LET THEM TALK,
   SOUL REBEL, TALK WON'T BOTHER ME.
I'M A CAPTURER, THAT'S WHAT THEY SAY,
   SOUL ADVENTURER, NIGHT AND DAY.
I'M A REBEL, SOUL REBEL.
  DO YOU HEAR THEM LIPPY.
I'M A CAPTURER, GOSSIP AROUND THE CORNER,
   SOUL ADVENTURER. HOW THEY ADVENTURE ON ME.

BUT, SEE THE MORNING SUN, THE MORNING SUN,
   ON THE HILLSIDE.
IF YOU'RE NOT LIVING GOOD, TRAVEL WIDE,
   YOU GOTTA TRAVEL WIDE.
SAID I'M A LIVING MAN,
  I'VE GOT WORK TO DO.
IF YOU'RE NOT HAPPY, THEN YOU MUST BE BLUE,
   MUST BE BLUE, PEOPLE SAY.

I'M A REBEL, SOUL REBEL.
I'M A CAPTURER, SOUL ADVENTURER.
DO YOU HEAR ME?
I'M A REBEL, REBEL IN THE MORNING.
SOUL REBEL, REBEL AT MIDDAY TIME.

Soul Rebel

Words and Music by Bob Marley

STIR IT UP

Words and Music by Bob Marley

Stir it up, little darling, stir it up.
Come on, baby, come on and stir it up, little darling,
   stir it up.
It's been a long, long time since I've got you on my mind.
And now you are here,
I say, it's so clear
To see what we can do, honey, just me and you.

Come on and stir it up, little darling, stir it up.
Come on baby, come on and stir it up, little darling,
   stir it up.
I'll push the wood, I'll blaze your fire,
Then I'll satisfy your heart's desire.
Said I'll stir it, yeah, ev'ry minute, yeah.
All you got to do is keep it in, baby.
And stir it up, little darling, stir it up.
Come on and stir it up, ooh, little darling, stir it up, yeah.

Oh, will you quench me while I'm thirsty?
Come and cool me down when I'm hot?
Your recipe, darling, is so tasty,
And you sure can stir your pot.
So stir it up, little darling, stir it up.
Come on and stir it up, ooh, little darling, stir it up.
Come on and stir it up, oh, little darling, stir it up.
Stir it up, little darling, stir it up.

(*Guitar Solo*)

Little darling, stir it up.
Come on and stir it up, little darling, stir it up.

STIR IT UP

Words and Music by Bob Marley

184

THANK YOU LORD

Words and Music by Bob Marley

THANK YOU, LORD, FOR WHAT YOU'VE DONE FOR ME.
THANK YOU, LORD, FOR WHAT YOU'RE DOING NOW.
THANK YOU, LORD, FOR EV'RY LITTLE THING.
THANK YOU, LORD, FOR YOU MADE ME SING.

SAY I'M IN NO COMPETITION,
BUT I MADE MY DECISION.
YOU CAN KEEP YOUR OPINION.
I'M JUST CALLING ON THE WISE MAN'S COMMUNION.

THANK YOU, LORD, FOR WHAT YOU'VE DONE FOR ME.
THANK YOU, LORD, FOR WHAT YOU'RE DOING NOW.
THANK YOU, LORD, FOR EV'RY LITTLE THING.
THANK YOU, LORD, FOR YOU MADE ME SING.

SING ALONG, SING ALONG.

I DON'T FEAR THEIR HUMILIATION,
JUST TO PROVE MY DETERMINATION.
I DON'T YIELD TO TEMPTATION,
I HAVEN'T LEARN'T MY LESSON IN REVELATION.

THANK YOU, LORD, FOR WHAT YOU'VE DONE FOR ME.
THANK YOU, LORD, FOR WHAT YOU'RE DOING NOW.
THANK YOU, LORD, FOR EV'RY LITTLE THING.
THANK YOU, LORD, FOR YOU MADE ME SING.

SING ALONG, SING ALONG.

(HORN SOLO)

SAY I'M IN NO COMPETITION
BUT I MADE MY DECISION,
LORD, IN MY SIMPLE WAY.
COMIN', COMIN', COMIN', COMIN'.
I LOVE TO PRAY.

THANK YOU, LORD, FOR WHAT YOU'VE DONE FOR ME.
THANK YOU, LORD, FOR WHAT YOU'RE DOING NOW.
THANK YOU, LORD, FOR EV'RY LITTLE THING.

Thank You Lord

Words and Music by Bob Marley

191

THREE LITTLE BIRDS

Words and Music by Bob Marley

DON'T WORRY ABOUT A THING,
'CAUSE EV'RY LITTLE THING GONNA BE ALRIGHT.
SINGIN', "DON'T WORRY ABOUT A THING,
'CAUSE EV'RY LITTLE THING GONNA BE ALRIGHT."
RISE UP THIS MORNING,
    SMILED WITH THE RISING SUN.
THREE LITTLE BIRDS PITCH BY MY DOORSTEP,
    SINGIN' SWEET SONGS OF MELODIES PURE AND TRUE,
SAYIN', "THIS IS MY MESSAGE TO YOU-U-U."
SINGIN'...
(REPEAT)

"DON'T WORRY ABOUT A THING,
'CAUSE EV'RY LITTLE THING GONNA BE AL-RIGHT."
(4 TIMES)

THREE LITTLE BIRDS

Words and Music by Bob Marley

WAITING IN VAIN

Words and Music by Bob Marley

I DON'T WANNA WAIT IN VAIN FOR YOUR LOVE.

I DON'T WANNA WAIT IN VAIN FOR YOUR LOVE.

FROM THE VERY FIRST TIME I BLESSED MY EYES ON YOU, GIRL,

MY HEART SAYS, "FOLLOW THROUGH."

BUT I KNOW NOW THAT I'M WAY DOWN ON YOUR LINE,

BUT THE WAITING FEEL IS FINE.

SO DON'T TREAT ME LIKE A PUPPET ON A STRING,

'CAUSE I KNOW HOW TO DO MY THING.

DON'T TALK TO ME AS IF YOU THINK I'M DUMB.

I WANNA KNOW WHEN YOU'RE GONNA COME.

SEE, I DON'T WANNA WAIT IN VAIN FOR YOUR LOVE.

I DON'T WANNA WAIT IN VAIN FOR YOUR LOVE.

I DON'T WANNA WAIT IN VAIN FOR YOUR LOVE.

'CAUSE IT'S SUMMER IS HERE,

I'M STILL WAITING THERE.

WINTER IS HERE AND I'M STILL WAITING THERE.

LIKE I SAID,

IT'S BEEN THREE YEARS SINCE I'M KNOCKIN' ON YOUR DOOR,

AND I STILL CAN KNOCK SOME MORE.

OOH, GIRL, OOH, GIRL,

IS IT FEASIBLE, I WANNA KNOW NOW,

FOR I TO KNOCK SOME MORE?

YA SEE, IN LIFE I KNOW THERE IS LOTS OF GRIEF,

BUT YOUR LOVE IS MY RELIEF.

TEARS IN MY EYES BURN,

TEARS IN MY EYES BURN WHILE I'M WAITING,

WHILE I'M WAITING FOR MY TURN.

SEE, I DON'T WANNA WAIT IN VAIN FOR YOUR LOVE.

I DON'T WANNA WAIT IN VAIN FOR YOUR LOVE.

I DON'T WANNA WAIT IN VAIN FOR YOUR LOVE.

I DON'T WANNA WAIT IN VAIN FOR YOUR LOVE.

I DON'T WANNA WAIT IN VAIN FOR YOUR LOVE.

OH, I DON'T WANNA, I DON'T WANNA,

I DON'T WANNA, I DON'T WANNA,

I DON'T WANNA WAIT IN VAIN.

NO, I DON'T WANNA, I DON'T WANNA,

I DON'T WANNA, I DON'T WANNNA,

I DON'T WANNA WAIT IN VAIN.

IT'S YOUR LOVE THAT I'M WAITING ON.

IT'S MY LOVE THAT YOU'RE RUNNING FROM.

(*REPEAT*)

Waiting In Vain

Words and Music by Bob Marley

WHO THE CAP FIT

Words and Music by Aston Barrett and Carlton Barrett

MAN TO MAN IS SO UNJUST, CHILDREN.
YOU DON'T KNOW WHO TO TRUST.
YOUR WORST ENEMY COULD BE YOUR BEST FRIEND,
AND YOUR BEST FRIEND YOUR WORST ENEMY.

SOME WILL EAT AND DRINK WITH YOU,
THEN BEHIND THEM SU-SU 'PON YOU.
ONLY YOUR FRIEND KNOW YOUR SECRETS,
SO ONLY HE COULD REVEAL IT.
AND WHO THE CAP FIT, LET THEM WEAR IT.
WHO THE CAP FIT, LET THEM WEAR IT.

SAID I THROW ME CORN,
ME NO CALL NO FOWL.
I SAYING,
"COK-COK-COK, CLUK-CLUCK-CLUCK," YEA!

SOME WILL HATE YOU,
PRETEND THEY LOVE YOU NOW.
THEN, BEHIND THEY TRY TO ELIMINATE YOU.
BUT WHO JAH BLESS, NO ONE CURSE.
THANK GOD, WE'RE PAST THE WORSE.

HYPOCRITES AND PARASITES
WILL COME UP AND TAKE A BITE.
AND IF YOUR NIGHT SHOULD TURN TO DAY,
A LOT OF PEOPLE WOULD RUN AWAY.
AND WHO THE CAP FIT, LET THEM WEAR IT.
WHO THE CAP FIT, LET THEM WEAR IT.

AND THEN A GONNA THROW ME CORN.
AND THEN A GONNA CALL NO FOWL.
AND THEN A GONNA
"COK-COK-COK, CLUK-CLUK-CLUK," YEA!

SOME WILL EAT AND DRINK WITH YOU.
THEN BEHIND THEM SU-SU 'PON YOU.
AND IF YOUR NIGHT SHOULD TURN TO DAY,
A LOT OF PEOPLE WOULD RUN AWAY.
AND WHO THE CAP FIT, LET THEM WEAR IT.
WHO THE CAP FIT, LET THEM WEAR IT.
I THROW ME CORN.
ME NO CALL NO FOWL.

I SAYING, "COK-COK-COK, CLUK-CLUK-CLUK."
(*REPEAT*)

WHO THE CAP FIT

Words and Music by Aston Barrett and Carlton Barrett

WHY SHOULD I

Words and Music by Bob Marley

WHY SHOULD I BEND DOWN MY HEAD AND CRY?
WHY SHOULD I BEND DOWN MY HEAD AND CRY?
THE OLD WORLD HAS ENDED,
    THE NEW WORLD HAS JUST BEGUN.
AND ALL THEM PEOPLE THAT LIVE THEREIN
    SHALL LIVE ON AND ON.
ONE MORE THING:
GOT TO GET WHAT I NEED,
GOT TO GET WHAT I WANT.
GOT TO GET WHAT I NEED,
GOT TO GET WHAT I WANT.
GOT TO GET SATISFACTION,
GOT TO GET THE ACTION.
GOT LOVE AND AFFECTION.
ONE MORE THING:

ONCE THERE WAS TWO ROADS BEFORE US
    TO PICK OUR CHOICE.
BUT GOOD HAS OVERCOME BAD.
THE SHEEP HAS HEARD THEIR MASTER'S VOICE.
SO TELL ME WHY.

WHY SHOULD I BEND DOWN MY HEAD AND CRY?
    NO REASON WHY.
WHY SHOULD I BEND DOWN MY HEAD AND CRY?
    (GOT TO MOVE) GOT TO GROOVE.

GOT TO GET WHAT I WANT.
WHAT DID YOU SAY?
GOT TO GET IT.
GOT TO GET WHAT I NEED.
GOT TO GET IT, TODAY NOW.
GOT TO GET WHAT I WANT.
LIKE I SAY, GOT TO GET IT.
GOT TO GET WHAT I NEED...SATISFACTION.

THE OLD WORLD HAS ENDED,
    THE NEW WORLD HAS JUST BEGUN.
AND ALL THEM PEOPLE THAT LIVE THEREIN
    SHALL LIVE ON AND ON.
ONE MORE THING:

WHY SHOULD I BEND DOWN MY HEAD AND CRY?
MY FATHER IS A KING.
WHY SHOULD I BEND DOWN MY HEAD AND CRY?
ALL THE RICHES IN THE EARTH.
SO TELL ME WHY,
WHY SHOULD I BEND DOWN MY HEAD AND CRY?

WHY SHOULD I

Words and Music by Bob Marley